D0720283

Presented to

_____

by

_____

on

_____

* * * * *

_____

_____

The Standard Publishing Company, Cincinnati, Ohio
A division of Standex International Corporation
© 1995 by The Standard Publishing Company
All rights reserved.
Printed in the United States of America
02 01 00 99 98 97 96 95   5 4 3 2 1

Library of Congress Catalog Card Number 95-8859
Cataloging-in-Publication data available
ISBN 0-7847-0331-0
RL 2.2

Devotions for Young Readers

52 Easy-to-Read Devotions With Activities

by Janet M. Bair
illustrated by Jenifer Schneider

STANDARD
PUBLISHING
Cincinnati, Ohio

Here's How to Use This Book

Now that you know how to read, you can read the Bible anytime, all by yourself. You don't have to wait for someone else to read it to you!

This book will help you read your Bible. It will help you think about Bible truths and your own life. It will help you spend some time with God each day.

There are 52 devotions, one for every week in the year. You can read them in order, or skip around and read what interests you. Here are some ideas for using one devotion each week:

• Each devotion has four pages. On the first day, read the first three pages.

• The next day, study the Bible verse on the last page of the devotion. Say it over and over until you know it. Write it out from memory.

• Another day, look up the Bible story. Use *The Young Reader's Bible,* if you have it. (If a story is long, read some of it each day.)

• Take some time each week to pray to God. The last page of each devotion has prayer ideas to help you.

• Have fun doing the activities.

After you learn the Bible verse, read the Bible story, use the prayer ideas, or do the activities, make a check mark inside the star beside that part. Check off the correct star on the Table of Contents (pages 6 and 7) whenever you complete all the parts of a devotion. This will be your record of how much you have learned!

There are other ways to use this book, too. You can do more than one devotion a week if you want to. You can do each devotion more than once. Instead of putting a check mark in the stars, you can put a little sticker over each star. (See page 224.)

You will find journal pages near the back of this book. You can use them to write out your favorite Bible verses or things you learn that you don't want to forget.

You will be surprised at how much of the Bible you can read! If you keep on reading, you will be amazed at how much you have read in a few months or a year!

Your word is like a lamp for my feet
and a light for my way.
Psalm 119:105

Table of Contents

Birthday Candles

When is your birthday?

Do you have a cake with candles?

Every year, you put

another candle on your cake.

Every year, you grow.

Jesus grew, too.

He grew taller and wiser.

When Jesus was twelve,

Mary and Joseph took him

to Jerusalem.

After the Passover feast,

Mary and Joseph headed home.

But Jesus was not with them!

They found him in the temple,

teaching the teachers!

Every year, you grow taller,

just like Jesus did.

And every year,

you can grow wiser, too.

You can know God better

and love God more.

That's what Jesus did.

A Verse to Learn

☆ Jesus continued to learn more
and more and to grow.
Luke 2:52

A Story to Read

☆ "Taller and Wiser"
on page 256 of *The Young Reader's Bible,*
or
☆ Luke 2:40-52

Something to Pray

☆ Ask God to help you
to know him better this year.

Something to Do

☆ Draw a picture of a cake with candles.
☆ For each year of your life, think of one thing
you have learned about God.

11

A New Start

Fall is here.

Time for school to start.

Time to get ready.

Lots of shopping to do.

New shoes. New lunch box.

New backpack.

New pencils and crayons.

The first day of school

is special. Exciting!

New teacher.

New children.

New classroom.

A chance to start over.

With God,

we can start over anytime.

We do not have to wait for fall.

When we've done

something wrong,

we can ask God to forgive us.

Because of Jesus,

God erases our sins,

just like an eraser

cleans a chalkboard at school.

The Bible says,*

"If anyone belongs to Christ,

then he is made new."

We can have a new life

with Jesus

any day!

*2 Corinthians 5:17

A Verse to Learn

☆ If anyone belongs to Christ,
then he is made new.
2 Corinthians 5:17

A Story to Read

☆ "Saul Sees the Light"
on page 412 of *The Young Reader's Bible*,
or
☆ Acts 9:1-22

Something to Pray

☆ Thank God for erasing all your sins.
☆ If you are starting a new school year, ask God
to help you make it a good one.

Something to Do

☆ Sharpen a new pencil. Use it to copy
2 Corinthians 5:17 on a new piece of paper.

Seasons

Every season brings fun times.

Rake a pile of leaves in the fall.

Jump into the pile!

Pick out a pumpkin.

When winter snow comes,

get out the sleds!

Build a snowman.

In the spring, put on your boots

and slosh through puddles.

Get out the kites and bikes!

Splash into summer.

Try to hit a home run!

Each season has its own

special games.

Winter, spring,

summer, and fall.

No matter where we live,

one season always changes

into another.

But God never changes.

He always stays the same.

He is always loving and kind.

He is always faithful to us!

A Verse to Learn

☆ Jesus Christ is the same yesterday,
today, and forever.
Hebrews 13:8

A Story to Read

☆ "Daniel for Dinner?"
on page 194 of *The Young Reader's Bible,*
or
☆ Daniel 6:16-28

Something to Pray

☆ Thank you, God, for the seasons. My favorite
is _____ . But I'm glad that *you* never change!

Something to Do

☆ What season is it now? Draw a picture
of a tree in that season.
☆ Make up a song about your favorite season.

19

The Rule of Love

Line up. Sit down.

Be quiet.

No running in the halls.

Raise your hand.

School rules!

God has his own rules, too.

They are the Ten Commandments

and the rule of love.

The Bible says,*

"We should love each other,

because love comes from God."

God helps us love other people.

Obeying school rules

keeps us out of trouble.

Obeying God's rule of love keeps

us from having "people trouble."

*1 John 4:7

There are a lot of people
who are hard to love.
Do you sometimes think,
"I don't like that kid. She lies."
Or, "He punches."
God does not love those sins,
but he does love those people.
God can show you
how to love those people, too.
You can smile, say something
kind, or share a candy bar.
God can give you
his love for anyone!

22

A Verse to Learn

☆ We love because God first loved us.
1 John 4:19

A Story to Read

☆ "A Neighbor Shows Kindness"
on page 316 of *The Young Reader's Bible,*
or
☆ Luke 10:30-37

Something to Pray

☆ Dear God, someone I know who is hard to
love is _____ . Help me think of a way
to show love to him or her.

Something to Do

☆ Play "Simon Says" with friends.
Follow the rules of the game.
☆ Obey the rules at school all week.

What's Inside Your Cereal Box?

Which cereal box

do you pick

in the store?

What's inside

your cereal box

this week?

A plastic toy

that changes color?

Stickers? A super ball?

It is fun to look forward

to finding the prize.

Sometimes you have to eat

a lot of cereal

to get it.

But cereal tastes good

and it's good for you, too!

25

When we read our Bibles,

we find lots of "prize" verses.

Sometimes we read

a lot of good verses

before we find a special verse.

But it is worth the wait!

Reading our special verses

is like hearing God talk

right to us!

Search your Bible

for "prize" verses,

just like you search

your cereal box!

A Verse to Learn

☆ God's word is alive and working.
Hebrews 4:12

A Story to Read

☆ "Jesus the Teacher"
on page 280 of *The Young Reader's Bible,*
or
☆ Matthew 7:24-27

Something to Pray

☆ Thank you, God, for the Bible. Please help me
find some "prize" verses.

Something to Do

☆ Ask a grown-up to tell you one of his or her
"prize" Bible verses.
☆ Make a bookmark for your Bible.
On it, write one Bible verse you like.

Lost and Found

School is a busy place!

It is easy to lose things at school.

You might lose your sweater,

your lunch box, or your backpack.

When that happens,

look in the "Lost and Found."

You might find what you had lost!

Jesus told a story about a man
who was lost and found.
He was "lost" when he left home
and did not follow God's ways.
He was "found"
when he came home again.
His father was still glad
to see him!

Without God's plans and words
to follow, we are lost.
When we believe in Jesus
as our Savior, we are "found"
like the man in the story.
Jesus is always glad
when someone new
believes in him. When we find out
about God's good ways
for our life,
it is a
happy day!

A Verse to Learn

☆ "My son . . . was lost,
but now he is found!"
Luke 15:24

A Story to Read

☆ "Lost and Found"
on page 328 of *The Young Reader's Bible,*
or
☆ Luke 15:11-32

Something to Pray

☆ Pray for someone you know
to believe in Jesus.

Something to Do

☆ Hide a toy. Have your friends hunt to find it.
The first one to find it yells,
"Huckle, Buckle Beanstalk!"

Recess Time

Balls bouncing.

Jump ropes turning.

Swinging and sliding.

Running and shouting.

Recess time is fun!

Recess is even more fun

if you have a friend

to play with you.

How do you make a friend?

Smile. Be kind.

Talk to someone new.

Ask him to play.

He may not know

you want to be

his friend!

Sometimes making friends is easy.

Sometimes it takes longer,

and we have to wait.

But there is one friend

we never have to wait for.

Jesus already wants to be

our friend!

Jesus loves us

and is with us

at recess time

and all the time!

A Verse to Learn

☆ "Now I call you friends."
John 15:15

A Story to Read

☆ "Jesus' Team of Twelve"
on page 268 of *The Young Reader's Bible*,
or
☆ Matthew 4:17-22

Something to Pray

☆ Thank you, Jesus, for being my friend! Help
me make a new friend this week, at school,
at church, or in my neighborhood.

Something to Do

☆ Try to make a new friend this week.
Ask someone who is not your friend
to play with you at recess or after school.

Lunchtime Traders

At lunchtime,

you may hear someone say,

"I will give you two cookies

for five fruit snacks."

Or, "I will trade my orange

for your brownie."

Trading and sharing lunches
can be fun
(as long as you eat
the sandwich
your mom packed!)

A long time ago,
a boy shared his lunch
with Jesus.
In the middle of a huge crowd,
the boy gave Jesus
five loaves of bread
and two small fish.

After Jesus prayed,

there was food for more than

five thousand hungry people!

There were twelve baskets

of leftovers, too —

all from one boy's little lunch!

We can share with Jesus, too.

We can give our time, our talents,

our money, and our things.

Jesus will use them

in great ways!

It is a good trade!

A Verse to Learn

✰ Use your gifts to serve each other.
1 Peter 4:10

A Story to Read

✰ "Enough for Everyone"
on page 298 of *The Young Reader's Bible,*
or
✰ John 6:1-13

Something to Pray

✰ Thank you, God, for all your gifts to me.
Help me to share what I have.

Something to Do

✰ Make a treat to eat
and share it with a friend.
✰ Look through your closet and drawers
for something someone else could use.

Time to Choose

Do you have a toy

or a hobby that you love

better than anything?

Could you live without it?

Is it more important to you

than God?

An idol is anything that we love
more than we love God.
It could be money, TV, sports,
or a hobby.
Elijah knew
a lot of people
who worshiped
an idol.
The idol
was called
Baal.

One day, Elijah said
to all the people,*
"If the Lord is the true God,
follow him."
Then God sent fire from heaven.
The people saw how great God is!
They wanted to obey him.

Do what Elijah said to do.
Make the choice.
Choose to love God,
not an idol.

*1 Kings 18:21

42

A Verse to Learn

☆ "Love the Lord your God with all
your heart, soul and strength."
Deuteronomy 6:5

A Story to Read

☆ "The Lord, He Is God!"
on page 170 of *The Young Reader's Bible,*
or
☆ 1 Kings 18:18-40

Something to Pray

☆ Tell God that you want to love him
most of all. Ask him to help you.

Something to Do

☆ Draw a heart. Print "God" in the center.
☆ Make a banner or poster for your wall
that says "GOD IS #1."

A Big God for Big Problems

Have you ever had

a big problem?

Do you have a friend

with a big problem?

Sometimes parents divorce.

A grandparent dies.

Your best friend moves away.

You have trouble

doing your schoolwork.

Jesus knows that children

can have big problems.

That is why he said,* "Let the

little children come to me."

He wants you to talk to him

about all your problems,

big *and* small.

*Matthew 19:14

When there is trouble at home,

or when you are very sad,

Jesus cares.

If you are having problems

at school,

Jesus cares.

The Bible says,*

"Give all your worries to him,

because he cares for you."

Our God will help us

with every problem,

no matter how big!

*1 Peter 5:7

46

A Verse to Learn

☆ Give all your worries to him,
because he cares for you.
1 Peter 5:7

A Story to Read

☆ "Let the Children Come"
on page 346 of *The Young Reader's Bible,*
or
☆ Mark 10:13-16

Something to Pray

☆ God, I'm glad you care about me and my
problems, big or small. Please help me
with this problem: _____ .

Something to Do

☆ Make a prayer list. Print your problems on one
side. Leave space to write in God's answers.

Substitute Teacher

After God took Elijah into heaven
in a chariot of fire,
Elisha took over Elijah's job
as a prophet.
When your real teacher is sick,
a substitute teacher takes over.
Some "subs" are nice.
Some are strict.
Some do not do things
the way your real teacher
does them.

48

Some kids want to goof off
when the real teacher isn't there.
"Why try hard?" they say.
"Who will know?"

But the Bible says,*

"Work as if you were working

for the Lord, not for men."

When you obey

your substitute teacher

and work hard,

you are pleasing the Lord.

Work hard,

no matter who is watching!

Be thankful when your

real teacher is back again!

*Colossians 3:23

A Verse to Learn

☆ Work as if you were working for the Lord,
not for men.
Colossians 3:23

A Story to Read

☆ "In a Chariot of Fire"
on page 176 of *The Young Reader's Bible,*
or
☆ 2 Kings 2:9-14

Something to Pray

☆ Pray for the substitute teachers
you see at your school this week.

Something to Do

☆ Play school at home. What is
your favorite subject?
☆ Pretend you are a substitute teacher.

51

Be a Thanks-Giver

What if you gave

your best friend a great present,

but your friend

never said thank-you?

How would you feel?

Ten men were sick
with a terrible skin disease.
Jesus healed all ten.
Only one man came back
to say thank-you to Jesus.
"Where are the other nine?"
asked Jesus.
Only one gave thanks!

Do we forget to thank God
for all he does for us?
How often should we thank him?
Every day!

We can thank God

for small things,

like colored leaves.

We can thank him for big things,

like healing someone we love.

The Bible says,* "Thank the Lord

because he is good.

His love continues forever."

Be a thanks-giver.

Don't forget!

*Psalm 107:1

A Verse to Learn

☆ Thank the Lord because he is good.
His love continues forever.
Psalm 107:1

A Story to Read

☆ "One Thankful Man"
on page 340 of *The Young Reader's Bible,*
or
☆ Luke 17:11-19

Something to Pray

☆ Thank God for the big and small
things he has done for you!

Something to Do

☆ Make place mats. Cut out pictures of things
you are thankful for. Glue them to construction
paper. Cover both sides with clear plastic.

Be a Music Maker

What is your favorite way

to make music?

Do you like to sing?

Do you play the piano,

or the violin, or the drums?

Long ago, David played the harp.
Maybe he learned to play it
while he watched his sheep.
David played his harp
for King Saul,
and the music helped the king
feel better.

God uses music to help us
in lots of ways.
Music can help us
get our feelings out.
Music can cheer us up.
And we can praise God
with music! The Bible tells us
to praise God with instruments,
dancing, and singing.
It doesn't have to be
only in church.
We can make music
and praise the Lord anywhere!

A Verse to Learn

☆ I will sing praises to my God as long as I live.
Psalm 146:2

A Story to Read

☆ "A New King for Israel"
on page 140 of *The Young Reader's Bible,*
or
☆ 1 Samuel 16:21-23

Something to Pray

☆ Ask God to help you to sing
a new song of your own.

Something to Do

☆ Make an instrument. Use a coffee can for a
drum. Put rice in containers for maracas. Tie
bells to a paper plate for a tambourine.
☆ March to music and praise the Lord!

Praise the Lord!

Christmas is a
time of surprises.
"What is in this package?"
"Who sent me this card?"

Mary was surprised by an angel.
The angel brought Mary
a message from God.
"You are going to have a baby!"
the angel said.
"He will be the Son of God."

Mary praised God for this news. "God has done great things for me," she said.

We can praise God

when we sing Christmas carols.

Think about the words.

Sing with all your heart!

We praise God

because of who he is

and what he does.

God is good to us!

He answers prayers every day.

He protects us.

He might even surprise us

with something amazing!

A Verse to Learn

☆ Let everything that breathes praise the Lord.
Psalm 150:6

A Story to Read

☆ "Mary Meets an Angel"
on page 226 of *The Young Reader's Bible,*
or
☆ Luke 1:46-55

Something to Pray

☆ Praise God for his kindness and love.
☆ Thank him for the things he has done for you.

Something to Do

☆ Make up a song about what God has done
for you. Or, sing your favorite carol.
☆ Use a clothespin and foil to make an angel.
Hang your angel on your Christmas tree.

No Room

Have you ever wanted tickets
to a baseball game, but they were
all sold out?
There was
no room left.

When Joseph and Mary came
to Bethlehem, the inn was full.
There was no room
for anyone else.
So Jesus was born in a stable.

Sometimes *people*

have no room for Jesus.

Our lives get too full

of sports, money, and toys.

Then we have no time

for talking with Jesus

or reading the Bible

or going to church.

But when we make room

for Jesus in our lives,

he can show us his love

and his great promises.

A Verse to Learn

☆ There were no rooms
left in the inn.
Luke 2:7

A Story to Read

☆ "One Night in Bethlehem"
on page 238 of *The Young Reader's Bible,*
or
☆ Luke 2:1-7

Something to Pray

☆ Tell Jesus that you want to always
have room for him in your life.

Something to Do

☆ Sing "Away in a Manger."
☆ Draw a picture of the stable with
baby Jesus in the manger.

Christmas Wish List

When a Christmas toy catalog

comes in the mail,

do you look at it and say,

"I want this and this and this"?

Your wish list gets

bigger and bigger!

God has a Christmas wish
for you! It is not for toys.
God's wish is better than toys.
The Bible says,* "God wants
all people to be saved."

*1 Timothy 2:4

69

For many years, God promised
to send a Savior to earth.
We can read these promises
in the Old Testament.
They all came true
when Jesus was born.
Jesus came to earth to save people
from their sins.
He is God's gift to us.

We all need to receive
God's Christmas gift to us —
Jesus!

A Verse to Learn

✮ For God loved the world so much
that he gave his only Son. . . . so that whoever
believes in him may . . . have eternal life.
John 3:16

A Story to Read

✮ "The Promised One"
on page 212 of *The Young Reader's Bible,*
or
✮ Isaiah 9:6, 7; Micah 5:2

Something to Pray

✮ Thank God for his Christmas wish
for you, and receive it!

Something to Do

✮ When you wrap gifts for Christmas,
think of Jesus, the best gift of all!

Look at That Star!

What are your favorite

Christmas decorations?

Do you put up lights

on your house?

Maybe you have a star

for the top of your tree.

There was a very special star
one night long ago.
The star was God's sign
that Jesus was born.
The star led the wise men to Jesus.
They worshiped Jesus
and gave him gifts.

What can we give to Jesus?

We can give him our love.

We can give him our time.

We can give him our songs

and the kind things

we do for others.

When you see star decorations

this Christmas,

remember the wise men.

Think of what you can give

to Jesus!

A Verse to Learn

☆ They gave him treasures of gold,
frankincense, and myrrh.
Matthew 2:11

A Story to Read

☆ "Follow That Star!"
on page 250 of *The Young Reader's Bible*,
or
☆ Matthew 2:1-12

Something to Pray

☆ Dear God, I want to give to Jesus this
Christmas. Help me think of a way.

Something to Do

☆ Make a star for your tree. Paint it yellow.
While the paint is wet, sprinkle on
a little salt or glitter to make it sparkle.

Jealous of Joseph

"It's not fair! You got the biggest
piece of pie.
You always get your own way!"
Do you hear yourself?
Are you ever jealous
of a brother or sister?

Joseph's brothers were jealous.

They did a terrible thing.

They sold their own brother

to be a slave in Egypt.

Everyone feels
jealous
sometimes.
When we

are jealous, we sometimes
feel like doing mean things.
What should we do
about these feelings?
Tell God right away.
Don't keep mean feelings inside.
Pray about the feelings.
Only God can take them away.
We just have to ask.

A Verse to Learn

☆ Do not be jealous or speak evil of others.
1 Peter 2:1

A Story to Read

☆ "Sold! A Sneaky Deal!"
on page 56 of *The Young Reader's Bible,*
or
☆ Genesis 37:3-28

Something to Pray

☆ Tell God about your jealous feelings.
Ask him to take them away.

Something to Do

☆ Draw a picture of Joseph's colorful coat.
☆ The next time you feel jealous,
make a list of things that you
are thankful for.

Trusting God for Good

Joseph was not free in Egypt.

He missed his father.

He had to learn a new language.

Then Joseph was sent to jail

for something he did not do.

But Joseph trusted God.

He waited for God to work.

And one day, Joseph became
a great ruler in Egypt!

Years later, Joseph's brothers
came to Egypt.
They needed food.
Joseph was kind and helped them.
He knew that God had worked
all things out for good.

Did you ever have to move?

Were you lonely?

You weren't the one

who wanted to move.

You wanted to go back

to your old house.

God can turn what seems

a bad thing into a good thing.

You might make better friends

than you had before!

Trust God for something good

in your new home, like Joseph!

A Verse to Learn

☆ Lord, I trust in you.
Psalm 31:1

A Story to Read

☆ "God Meant It for Good"
on page 68 of *The Young Reader's Bible,*
or
☆ Genesis 45:1-12

Something to Pray

☆ Ask God to help you trust him for
something good in a bad place.

Something to Do

☆ Pretend to be Joseph. Be kind
to your family today.
☆ Find Jeremiah 29:11 in your Bible.
Read what good plans God has for you!

Hide and Seek

"One, two, three, four, five,

six, seven, eight, nine, ten.

Ready or not, here I come!"

Hide-and-seek is a fun game.

The other child

looks and looks and looks.

Maybe he finds you.

Maybe not!

But there is someone

who always knows where you are.

God. The Bible says,*

"You know where I go

and where I lie down.

You know well

everything I do."

*Psalm 139:3

God sees us when we are

at the mall,

at a sleep-over party,

or on a hike.

Even if we do something so bad

that we want to run away

from God, we can't.

God still sees us

and wants to forgive us.

We can never play hide-and-seek

with God.

He will always find us!

A Verse to Learn

☆ You are all around me —
in front and in back.
Psalm 139:5

A Story to Read

☆ "The King Who Sang Praises"
on page 152 of *The Young Reader's Bible,*
or
☆ Psalm 139:1-18

Something to Pray

☆ Thank God for always being able
to find you (even if you get lost).

Something to Do

☆ Find a dark place to hide, just for fun.
☆ While you are hiding, talk to God.
Remember that he still sees you!

Wise Like Solomon

Have you ever heard anyone say,
"That was a dumb thing
for me to do"?
We all say that sometimes.
We need God's wisdom
to do wise things.

King Solomon knew
he needed God's wisdom.
God spoke to Solomon
in a dream. God said,*
"Ask for anything you want.
I will give it to you."
Solomon asked for wisdom
to rule his people well. *1 Kings 3:5

God made Solomon
a very wise king.
Solomon knew how to do
the right thing
at the right time.
The Bible says,* "If any of you
needs wisdom,
you should ask God for it."
God wants us to ask.
God will help us
to be wise like Solomon!

*James 1:5

A Verse to Learn

☆ Only the Lord gives wisdom.
Proverbs 2:6

A Story to Read

☆ "Solomon's One Wish"
on page 158 of *The Young Reader's Bible,*
or
☆ 1 Kings 3:5-14

Something to Pray

☆ Thank God for helping you to grow wiser
every day.

Something to Do

☆ Plan a treasure hunt for a friend.
Hide your Bible as the treasure.
☆ Count how many times the word *wisdom*
is used in Proverbs 2 in your Bible.

A Watchful Helper

Miriam was Moses' big sister.
She watched baby Moses
in his basket on the river.
She waited and watched,
and she found a way to help.
Miriam brought Moses' own
mother to care for him!

You can be a watchful helper
at home.
You can watch a younger child.
Run after him to keep him safe.
Keep sharp things out of reach.
Don't let him eat
sand in the sandbox!

You can help by watching a pet.

Don't let the puppy

chew on anyone's shoes.

Don't let the cat

scratch the chairs

with his claws.

Always give your pet

plenty of water and food.

You can be a watchful helper.

And if you need help,

God will help *you!*

A Verse to Learn

✰ Try to do what is good for each other.
1 Thessalonians 5:15

A Story to Read

✰ "Baby Moses' Riverboat"
on page 74 of *The Young Reader's Bible,*
or
✰ Exodus 2:1-10

Something to Pray

✰ Tell God you want to be a watchful helper
at home. Ask him to help you see ways
you can help.

Something to Do

✰ Make a list of ways to be a helper in
your family or at school or church.
✰ Surprise someone with your help.

Playing Tag

"Not it."

"Not it."

"You're it."

No one wants to be "it"

in the game of tag.

Some kids are hard to catch!

Moses did not want

to be "it" —

the man to lead God's people

out of Egypt. But God said,*

"I will be with you."

God's promise was enough!

*Exodus 3:12

Sometimes you are chosen

to do a hard job,

like cleaning the basement

or the birdcage.

You wish you could say

"not it" and get out of the job!

But when you are asked

to do a hard job,

God will help you.

That is the best help

in the world!

A Verse to Learn

☆ God said, "I will be with you."
Exodus 3:12

A Story to Read

☆ "I Am Sending You"
on page 80 of *The Young Reader's Bible,*
or
☆ Exodus 3:1-12

Something to Pray

☆ Thank the Lord for helping you
to do hard jobs, just like he helped Moses.

Something to Do

☆ Play a game of tag with some friends.
Think about Moses when you are "it."
☆ Surprise your parents by doing a hard job
around the house without being asked.

Moses' Mountain Message

Have you ever been

on top of a high hill

or a mountain?

The world looks so big!

The Bible says,*

"I look up to the hills.

But where does my help

come from?

My help comes from the Lord."

*Psalm 121:1, 2

Moses went up a mountain
to talk to God.
God gave Moses
ten rules for living.
We call these rules
the Ten Commandments.
God wrote the rules
on two stone tablets.

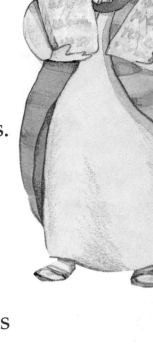

The Ten Commandments
show us the right way to live,
even today!

A Verse to Learn

☆ My help comes from the Lord.
Psalm 121:2

A Story to Read

☆ "A Special Treasure"
on page 98 of *The Young Reader's Bible,*
or
☆ Exodus 20:1-17

Something to Pray

☆ Thank God for giving us his commandments.
Ask him to help you learn and obey them.

Something to Do

☆ Use clay or play dough to make two tablets
like God gave to Moses.
☆ Recite any of the Ten Commandments
that you know. Learn a new one.

Waiting With Joshua

"Line up, everyone,"
the teacher calls.
There is a line
for going to recess.
There is a line
for going to lunch.
There is a line
for getting on the bus
at the end of the day.
Sometimes waiting in line
is boring!

God told Joshua to march his army in a line around Jericho.

They marched for seven days,

with no talking at all!

On the seventh day, Joshua said,*

"Now, shout!

The Lord has given you this city!"

The walls of Jericho fell down!

Joshua and the people had waited.

God helped them in a big way!

We can wait patiently just like

Joshua, in any line, anywhere!

*Joshua 6:16

A Verse to Learn

☆ Wait for the Lord's help.
Psalm 27:14

A Story to Read

☆ "Seven Times and a Shout"
on page 110 of *The Young Reader's Bible,*
or
☆ Joshua 6:1-20

Something to Pray

☆ Ask God to help you to wait patiently
like Joshua, in line or anytime.

Something to Do

☆ Build a city with blocks. Put a wall around it.
March some toy people around it seven times.
☆ Look at the days of a week on a calendar.
Think about how long seven days is.

A Good Listener

Does your teacher ever say,

"Now listen, class"?

When you hear that,

you know the teacher

is getting ready

to tell you something

you need to know.

We have to listen
in order to learn.
God spoke to Samuel
in the dark.
At first, Samuel did not know
who was calling him.
But he learned
to listen to God.
And God told Samuel
what he wanted
Samuel
to know.

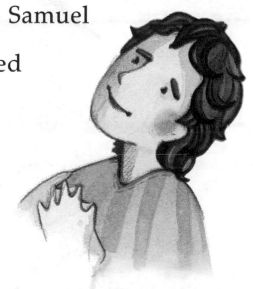

We can listen to God, too.

God is talking to us

when we read a Bible verse

or sing a Bible song

or hear a Bible story.

God's words are true words.

They are always helpful.

We can be good listeners,

like Samuel.

We can learn to listen to God.

A Verse to Learn

☆ Samuel said, "Speak, Lord. . . . I am listening."
1 Samuel 3:10

A Story to Read

☆ "A Voice in the Dark"
on page 134 of *The Young Reader's Bible,*
or
☆ 1 Samuel 3:1-18

Something to Pray

☆ Tell God that you want to be a good listener.
Ask him to help you learn to listen to his Word.

Something to Do

☆ Listen to a Bible song on a tape or CD.
Sing along if you would like to.
☆ If you have *The Young Reader's Bible Audio
Cassette*, listen to a Bible story.

Learning Like Timothy

Do you like to learn new things?

New songs? New jokes?

New riddles? New games?

New animal facts? Do you like

to learn new sports?

Do you like to learn
new Bible verses?
Timothy did.
He learned Bible verses
from his mother
and his grandmother.

When he got older,

Timothy learned about God

from his friend Paul.

Paul wrote two letters

to Timothy. They are found

in the New Testament.

God loves for us to learn his Word!

The Bible teaches us how to live

and act God's way.

You can be

a good learner,

like Timothy!

A Verse to Learn

☆ The Scriptures are able to make you wise.
2 Timothy 3:15

A Story to Read

☆ "Timothy Joins the Journey"
on page 418 of *The Young Reader's Bible,*
or
☆ 2 Timothy 1:2-5

Something to Pray

☆ Ask God to help you learn his Word,
like Timothy.

Something to Do

☆ In your Bible, find Paul's letters to Timothy.
☆ Think of something new
you would like to learn.
☆ Ask someone to help you learn it.

115

Push That Play Dough!

Playing with play dough is fun!

You can press it.

You can punch it.

You can poke it.

You can push it.

You can shape it

any way you want.

It is fun to make things!

God made us. The Bible says,*

"We are like clay,

and you are the potter."

A potter makes things out of clay.

He shapes clay just like

you shape play dough.

God made us.

He shapes our lives

by teaching us his ways.

He helps us to be

more like him!

*Isaiah 64:8

A Verse to Learn

☆ God created human beings in his image.
Genesis 1:27

A Story to Read

☆ "The Beginning"
on page 14 of *The Young Reader's Bible,*
or
☆ Genesis 1:1-31

Something to Pray

☆ Thank God for creating you.
☆ Ask God to help you
to be more like him.

Something to Do

☆ Play with some play dough. Make something
new. Think about how God made you and
shapes you.

Zoo View

What animals do you like best?

The monkeys? The otters?

The tigers? The bears?

God made so many kinds

of animals!

Adam, the first man,

gave all the animals their names.

But Adam still felt alone.

The animals could not

talk to him.

So God made Eve.

Then Adam

was

happy.

We can have fun with animals.

We love our pets.

Animals help people work
and travel.

Animals give us food.

God gave us all the animals.

But we need other *people*, too.

We need families and friends.

We need teachers and doctors.

Everyone who is special to you
is someone God made.

Our God knows what we need.

He is a smart God!

A Verse to Learn

✰ God said, "It is not good for the man to be alone." *Genesis 2:18*

A Story to Read

✰ "Man and Woman"
on page 20 of *The Young Reader's Bible,*
or
✰ Genesis 2:18-23

Something to Pray

✰ Thank God for a special animal.
✰ Thank God for the people you love.

Something to Do

✰ Play zoo with your toy animals.
✰ Cut out pictures of animals. Pretend you are Adam and make up new names for them.
✰ Play with a special friend.

The Cross and Our Sins

"Stop hitting me!"

"You hit me first."

Have you ever been punished

for fighting?

What was your punishment?

Time out? Grounding?

Extra chores?

There is another kind
of punishment. The Bible says,*
"When someone sins,
he earns what sin pays — death.
But God gives us a free gift —
life forever."
Everyone sins.
Everyone earns death.
But Jesus died on the cross
so that God would not
have to give us
that punishment!

*Romans 6:23

When Jesus is our Savior,
God forgives our sins.
Our bodies will die someday,
but we will live forever with God
and Jesus because of what Jesus
did for us on the cross.

126

A Verse to Learn

☆ Christ himself died for you. And that
one death paid for your sins.
1 Peter 3:18

A Story to Read

☆ "King of a Different Kingdom"
on page 376 of *The Young Reader's Bible,*
or
☆ Mark 15:20-39

Something to Pray

☆ Tell Jesus you are sorry for your sins.
☆ Thank him for dying on the cross for you.

Something to Do

☆ Draw a cross. Write the sins that you know
you have done on the cross. If Jesus is your
Savior, God has forgiven you!

He Is Alive!

On Easter Sunday,

all around the world,

people are glad.

There are colorful Easter baskets,

Easter eggs, and flowers.

People wear bright new clothes.

Why do we celebrate Easter?

Jesus is risen from the dead!

When the women

went to the tomb,

it was empty!

Later, the women

and the disciples saw Jesus alive.

How glad they were!

Jesus wants his followers

to tell everyone

that he died for our sins

and that he is alive again.

We can send Easter cards

to tell others that Jesus lives!

We can smile and sing

and tell our friends

that Jesus lives!

Like the angels

at the empty tomb,

we can say,

"He has risen!"

A Verse to Learn

☆ "Jesus is not here. He has risen!"
Luke 24:6

A Story to Read

☆ "Could It Be True?"
on page 382 of *The Young Reader's Bible,*
or
☆ Luke 24:1-12

Something to Pray

☆ Thank God that Jesus is alive.
He has risen!

Something to Do

☆ Make two paper-plate puppets. Draw a sad
face on one. Put a happy face on the other.
☆ Then do a puppet show about how people
felt on the first Easter morning.

131

Picnic Time

What do you like to eat

at a picnic?

Sandwiches or hot dogs?

Chips or salads?

Cookies or watermelon?

Everything tastes so good!

The prophet Elijah had many
"picnic" breakfasts and suppers.
Ravens brought bread and meat
to Elijah as he hid
from King Ahab.
Elijah must have been thankful
to see those ravens every day!
God was taking care of Elijah.

Food is one of God's gifts to us.

Are you thankful for your food?

Do you eat foods

that are good for you?

Learn to try new foods.

Sometimes you are served food

you don't like.

You can still eat some of it

politely and not complain.

God wants a thankful heart,

at everyday meals

and at picnic time!

A Verse to Learn

✫ Always give thanks to God the Father
for everything.
Ephesians 5:20

A Story to Read

✫ "Meals for the Messenger"
on page 164 of *The Young Reader's Bible,*
or
✫ 1 Kings 17:1-6

Something to Pray

✫ Thank God for your favorite picnic food.

Something to Do

✫ Make a healthy snack. Eat it outside. Share
with a friend. Thank God for your food.
✫ If it's raining, have your picnic indoors
on a blanket!

Bullies on the Bus

Is there a mean kid, a bully,

on your bus or on your street?

Is there someone at school

who just won't leave you alone?

What should you do?

David faced a big bully,

a Philistine named Goliath.

He was a mean giant,

nine feet tall!

But David trusted God.

David was only a boy,

but God used him.

God helped David fight Goliath
because God's people
and the Philistines were at war.
When a bully is mean to you,
try not to *have* to fight.
Jesus said,* "Love your enemies.
Pray for those who hurt you."
Pray to God, be brave like David,
and God will work out
your troubles *his* way!

*Matthew 5:44

138

A Verse to Learn

☆ "Love your enemies. Pray for those
who hurt you."
Matthew 5:44

A Story to Read

☆ "A Giant Problem"
on page 146 of *The Young Reader's Bible,*
or
☆ 1 Samuel 17:32-37

Something to Pray

☆ Ask the Lord to help you be brave like David.
☆ If you know a mean kid, pray for him or her.

Something to Do

☆ Draw a picture of a school bus.
God is watching over you
when you ride your bus.

Brave Like Esther

Esther was a pretty Jewish girl who became the queen of Persia. An evil man wanted to kill all the Jews in the kingdom.

Esther knew

she had to ask the king

not to kill the Jews.

Long ago in Persia,

if the queen went to the king

and he did not want to see her,

she could be killed.

But Esther was brave.

She said, "If I die, I die."

God was with Esther.

The king was happy to see her.

All of the Jews were safe

in the kingdom of Persia.

God wants us

to be brave and to trust him,

just like Esther did.

God will help you to be brave

when you go to the doctor's

for a shot.

Or when you learn

to swim and dive.

Or when you go

to a new school.

Whenever you are afraid,

God will help you

to be brave.

A Verse to Learn

☆ Be strong and brave.
Psalm 31:24

A Story to Read

☆ "A Plan and a Party"
on page 200 in *The Young Reader's Bible,*
or
☆ Esther 4:8-16

Something to Pray

☆ Tell God about the times you are afraid.
Ask him to help you be brave.

Something to Do

☆ Make two paper-bag puppets,
a king and a queen.
☆ Use your puppets to tell the story of Esther
in your own words.

Building Blocks

You can find all kinds of blocks.

Wooden blocks.

Lincoln logs. Duplos and Legos.

What can you build with blocks?

Almost anything!

Towers. Bridges. Churches.

Roads. And walls!

Nehemiah was a builder.

He helped rebuild the walls

around Jerusalem.

Enemies tried to stop him.

But God helped Nehemiah.

God helped the people

work along with Nehemiah.

Together they got the job done.

Nehemiah was a man
who did not give up.
He finished the job God gave him.
You can be like Nehemiah.
When you do chores at home,
finish them!
Clean *all* of your room,
even under the bed!
You may have a hard job
like raking leaves
or shoveling snow.
Don't give up! God will help
you finish your work!

A Verse to Learn

☆ "The God of heaven will give us success."
Nehemiah 2:20

A Story to Read

☆ "Remember and Obey"
on page 206 of *The Young Reader's Bible,*
or
☆ Nehemiah 2:11-20

Something to Pray

☆ Ask God to help you finish your work
like Nehemiah did.
☆ Ask God to help you not to give up
when work is hard.

Something to Do

☆ With blocks, make a wall like Nehemiah did.
☆ Try something new that is hard. Don't give up!

Running Races

Do you like to race?

Some board games are races.

Can you be the first to the finish?

Running races are fun, too.

How fast can you go?

There are lots
of running games to play.
In "Red Rover,"
you run to break through
the other team's wall.

The Bible says,*

"Let us run the race

that is before us

and never give up."

Our life is like a race to heaven

to be with Jesus forever.

If we keep on loving Jesus,

we will win our race of faith.

That will be better

than any race or game

we ever win here on earth.

*Hebrews 12:1

A Verse to Learn

☆ Let us run the race that is before us
and never give up.
Hebrews 12:1

A Story to Read

☆ "Parting Promises"
on page 394 of *The Young Reader's Bible,*
or
☆ Revelation 21:1-4

Something to Pray

☆ Ask Jesus to help you to love him
and to win your race of faith.

Something to Do

☆ Play a board game or a running game.
As you play, think about running
to be with Jesus.

Transforming Toys

Did you ever see a toy

become something else?

A car transforms into a robot.

A man transforms

into a superhero.

Zaccheus changed
when he met Jesus.
He had been a cheater
and a thief.
But after he knew Jesus,
Zaccheus wanted to be honest.
He paid back everyone
he had cheated.

Jesus wants to transform us.

He wants to help us

do what is right.

He wants to help us

be more like him.

As we listen to God's Word

and obey it,

we become more like Jesus.

Every day we decide.

Do we obey?

Or do we not?

Jesus can transform us

if we let him!

A Verse to Learn

☆ We are being changed to be like him.
2 Corinthians 3:18

A Story to Read

☆ "Big News for a Little Man"
on page 352 of *The Young Reader's Bible,*
or
☆ Luke 19:1-10

Something to Pray

☆ Tell Jesus you want to be
more like him.
☆ Ask him to change you.

Something to Do

☆ Play with a transforming toy, if you have one.
☆ Or draw a picture of a transforming toy
that you would like to make.

Jesus Stills the Storm

A lake in summer seems so quiet.

Little waves of water

lap the shore.

But when a storm comes,

the waves grow big.

You do not want to be out

in a boat in a storm!

One night, a big storm began
when Jesus was asleep in a boat.
The disciples were afraid.
They woke Jesus up.
Jesus told the wind and waves
to be still, and the
storm stopped!

The disciples were glad.

They said,*

"Even the wind and the sea

obey him!"

Jesus has power

over all things.

If you are ever afraid

in a storm, remember —

Jesus has great power

to keep you safe!

*Matthew 8:27

A Verse to Learn

☆ "Even the wind and the sea obey him!"
Matthew 8:27

A Story to Read

☆ "Wild Winds and Waves Obey"
on page 292 of *The Young Reader's Bible,*
or
☆ Matthew 8:23-27

Something to Pray

☆ Thank Jesus for his great power.
☆ Are you afraid of something now? Ask Jesus
to help you and keep you safe.

Something to Do

☆ In the bathtub or a sink, make a pretend
storm. Make the storm stop.
(Clean up your mess, too!)

Mud-Puddle Fun

Rain brings puddles.

Puddles make mud.

Mud squishes. Mud oozes.

You can make mud pies,

mud pancakes, mud meatballs,

mud forts, and mud castles.

Even Jesus used mud.
He used it in a special way
to heal a blind man's eyes.
Jesus used everyday things
in extra-special ways.

Jesus wants to use *you*

in special ways, too.

You may feel ordinary,

like mud,

but Jesus can use you!

He can use you

to pray for others,

to cheer others up,

to help others in need.

And Jesus can use you

to tell others about him!

A Verse to Learn

☆ Never become tired of doing good.
2 Thessalonians 3:13

A Story to Read

☆ "Now I See"
on page 310 of *The Young Reader's Bible,*
or
☆ John 9:1-7

Something to Pray

☆ Ask God to use you to help others
in an extra-special way.

Something to Do

☆ Play with some mud or clay.
Be sure to clean up your mess!
☆ Draw a picture of what the blind man
saw after he was healed.

Faithful Friends

What is a faithful friend?

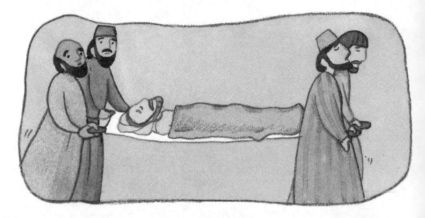

Four friends brought

their sick friend to Jesus.

He could not walk,

so his four friends

carried him on a mat.

They knew Jesus could heal him.

It was too crowded to see Jesus.

But the four friends

were faithful.

They did not give up.

They did not go home.

They lowered their friend

through the roof to see Jesus.

Jesus healed their friend,

and they all walked home!

You can be a faithful friend.

If your friend is sick,

you can pray.

If your friend is worried,

you can listen.

If your friend misses school,

you can bring her

the homework assignment.

If someone makes fun

of your friend,

you can speak up for him.

Even when it is hard,

you can be a faithful friend!

A Verse to Learn

☆ A friend loves you all the time.
Proverbs 17:17

A Story to Read

☆ "Inside and Out"
on page 274 of *The Young Reader's Bible,*
or
☆ Mark 2:1-12

Something to Pray

☆ Tell God that you want to be a faithful friend.
Ask him to show you what to do.

Something to Do

☆ Make a get-well card. Send it
to someone who is sick.
☆ Call a friend on the phone, just to say
"I was thinking about you."

Teach Us to Pray

Jesus taught his friends
how to pray.
He gave them a special prayer
for an example.
Sometimes Jesus' prayer is called
"The Lord's Prayer."
It is a good one to learn.

We can pray our own prayers, too.
Did you know that we can talk
to God

about

anything?

We can tell God how we feel.

We can ask for what we need.

We can pray for friends

to know Jesus,

and for sick people to get well.

We can thank God for answers

even before they come!

God hears us when we pray,

and he loves to answer us.

A Verse to Learn

☆ Pray with all kinds of prayers.
Ephesians 6:18

A Story to Read

☆ "Teach Us to Pray"
on page 322 of *The Young Reader's Bible,*
or
☆ Matthew 6:9-13

Something to Pray

☆ Thank God for hearing and answering
our prayers.

Something to Do

☆ Choose a place in your room or in your house
to be your special prayer place.
☆ Start learning the Lord's Prayer if you don't
already know it by heart.

News for the Whole World

The world is such a big place!

There are many nations,

many tribes,

many ways of speaking.

There are many people

who have never heard of Jesus

or God or the Bible.

God told Jonah to go to Nineveh.

The people there

did not know God.

Jonah didn't want to go,

and he ran away.

But later, Jonah changed his mind.

He obeyed God

and preached in Nineveh,

and God saved the city.

Sometimes we might not *feel*

like obeying God.

We might not *feel*

like caring about

the needs of others.

But if we do it anyway,

God can do mighty things,

just like he did in Nineveh!

A Verse to Learn

☆ Pray that the Lord's teaching
will continue to spread quickly.
2 Thessalonians 3:1

A Story to Read

☆ "A Gulp and a Great City"
on page 182 of *The Young Reader's Bible,*
or
☆ Jonah 3:1-10

Something to Pray

☆ Ask God to send his Word to many nations.
☆ Ask God how you can help.

Something to Do

☆ Look at a world map. Choose seven different
countries. Every day this week, pray for the
people in one of those countries.

The Great Name of Jesus

Your parents thought a lot
about the name
they picked for you.
They wanted it to be special,
just for you.

176

The Bible says,*

"God made the name of Christ

greater than every other name."

There is power in the name

of Jesus! If we belong to Jesus,

we can pray to God

in Jesus' name.

Philippians 2:9

When you need help,

you must ask the right person.

When your bike needs fixing,

you don't go to the pet shop.

When you need to learn to swim,

you don't go to the grocery store.

You go where you will get

the help you need.

When we need

a prayer answered,

we can go to God

in Jesus' name!

A Verse to Learn

☆ God made the name of Christ
greater than every other name.
Philippians 2:9

A Story to Read

☆ "Just Say the Word"
on page 286 in *The Young Reader's Bible,*
or
☆ Philippians 2:9-11

Something to Pray

☆ Thank God for the power in Jesus' name.
☆ Thank him that we can pray in Jesus' name.

Something to Do

☆ Print the name "JESUS" as fancy
as you can. Use lots of colors.
Hang it up and look at it often.

Show and Tell

Did you ever have "Show and Tell" time in your class at school?

What did you show?

What did you tell?

Did you share something from nature?

Did you tell about a book

you had read?

Did you show a new toy?

You had to stand up

in front of your class and talk.

Did you feel a little shy?

Paul and Silas were not shy.

They preached boldly about Jesus.

Sometimes their preaching

got them in trouble.

But Paul could not stop

preaching about Jesus.

He wanted to tell the world

what Jesus had done in his life.

Can we "show and tell" Jesus

to our friends?

Yes! We can tell them

the great things

Jesus has done for us.

A Verse to Learn

☆ "We must speak about
what we have seen and heard."
Acts 4:20

A Story to Read

☆ "The Night the Prison Shook"
on page 424 of *The Young Reader's Bible,*
or
☆ Acts 16:16-35

Something to Pray

☆ Ask God to help you tell others about Jesus.

Something to Do

☆ Think of a friend who doesn't know about
Jesus. Draw a picture, write a note,
or call your friend on the phone. Invite her
to Sunday school or a church activity.

Dress-Up Time

It is fun to play dress-up!

It is fun to pretend to be a doctor,

a fire fighter, a dancer,

or a clown. But did you know

the Bible tells us

to "dress up" like soldiers, too?

The Bible says,*

"Wear the full armor of God."

What is this armor?

First, there is the **belt of truth.**

God's Word is truth.

We want to know

what God's Word says.

Next comes the **breastplate**

of righteousness.

Doing what is right

will keep us safe

from many problems.

Ephesians 6:11

185

For **shoes**, we wear

the good news about Jesus.

They make us ready to tell others

how Jesus brings peace.

Our **shield** is faith.

Our **helmet** is salvation,

and our **sword** is God's Word.

Satan always wants

to cause us trouble,

but God keeps us safe

when we have our armor on!

186

A Verse to Learn

☆ Wear the full armor of God.
Ephesians 6:11

A Story to Read

☆ "Peter Takes a Walk" (about having faith)
on page 304 of *The Young Reader's Bible,*
or
☆ Ephesians 6:10-17

Something to Pray

☆ Thank God for his armor
and for keeping you safe.

Something to Do

☆ Draw a shield. Write "FAITH" on it.
☆ Play dress-up. What can you
pretend to be?
☆ Sing "I'm in the Lord's Army."

Sharing the Good News

We like to jump!

Jump playing hopscotch.

Jump rope. Jump over puddles.

Jump into leaves.

Jump on the bed!

Peter and John saw a man

who could not jump.

He could not even walk.

Peter said,* "By the power

of Jesus — stand up and walk!"

The man stood up.

He walked! He jumped!

And he praised God!

Acts 3:6

Peter loved to share
the Good News of Jesus.
Do you? You can say,
"Jesus loves you.
He can heal you.
He can protect you.
He has a good plan
for your life."
Any news about Jesus
is good news!

A Verse to Learn

☆ The Good News . . . is the power God uses
to save everyone who believes.
Romans 1:16

A Story to Read

☆ "Jumping for Joy"
on page 406 of *The Young Reader's Bible,*
or
☆ Acts 3:1-10

Something to Pray

☆ Ask God to help you tell the Good News
about Jesus to a friend.

Something to Do

☆ Pretend you are the man Jesus healed.
Imagine how he felt and
jump for joy five times!

Helping Like Dorcas

From the TV news,

we know that there are

many poor people in our world.

How can just one person

help them?

God wants us to give to others.

The Bible says,*

"Give freely to the poor

and needy in your land."

Dorcas was a person

who helped poor people.

She sewed lots of shirts and coats.

She was always very busy

helping

others.

*Deuteronomy 15:11

193

You may not know

how to sew coats like Dorcas.

But could you collect cans

and give the money?

Could you plant a garden

and give the vegetables

to a shelter?

Could you clean out your closet

and give the clothes

that are too small

to someone who needs them?

You can find a way

to help like Dorcas did.

A Verse to Learn

☆ "Give freely to the poor and needy
in your land."
Deuteronomy 15:11

A Story to Read

☆ "Ruth's Rich Reward" (how Ruth helped)
on page 128 of *The Young Reader's Bible,*
or
☆ Acts 9:36-42 (about Dorcas)

Something to Pray

☆ Ask God to help you help someone in need.

Something to Do

☆ Look for "buy one, get one free" coupons
to cut out for your mom or dad. Ask if
you may give the free items to a food bank
in your town or at church.

195

Things to Remember

There are lots of things

to remember!

Brush your teeth,

twice every day.

Comb your hair. Feed your pet.

Don't forget!

Do you ever forget?

On the night before he died,

Jesus shared a special dinner

with his disciples.

Jesus said, "Remember me."

He knew it is easy

to get busy

and forget.

In churches today,

we remember Jesus

as he told us to do.

We call this time

"communion."

It is a time to remember

what Jesus did for us

on the cross.

All over the world,

people remember Jesus

  during communion!

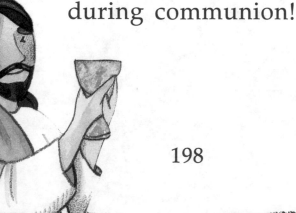

A Verse to Learn

☆ "Do this to remember me."
Luke 22:19

A Story to Read

☆ "Remember Me"
on page 364 of *The Young Reader's Bible,*
or
☆ Mark 14:22-25

Something to Pray

☆ Thank Jesus for what he has done for you.

Something to Do

☆ Make a list of the things
you need to remember every day.
Put Jesus at the top!
☆ During communion,
say your own prayer.

Surprises

Do you like surprises?

When someone gives a gift to you,

you can hardly wait to open it!

God likes to give surprises

to his people.

Abraham had no children.

He was an old man.

His wife, Sarah, was old, too.

But God promised him a son.

Abraham waited a long time.

When Abraham was 100,

his son Isaac was born.

What a great surprise from God!

God may have surprises for you.

What you grow up to be

might surprise you.

A missionary? A preacher?

A singer? A teacher?

Where you live someday

may be a surprise.

Maybe you will live

in a foreign country.

Trust God with your life,

like Abraham did.

You will find that God

has good surprises for you.

A Verse to Learn

☆ "Is anything too hard for the Lord?"
Genesis 18:14

A Story to Read

☆ "A Surprise for Sarah"
on page 38 in *The Young Reader's Bible,*
or
☆ Genesis 21:5-7

Something to Pray

☆ Ask God to help you grow up to be what
he wants you to be.

Something to Do

☆ Pretend you are grown up. What would you
like the most to be?
☆ Look at a world map. Where do you think
you will live someday?

Bedtime Buddies

Do you ever sleep

with a toy at night?

Maybe you have a cuddly bear

or a bunny.

Maybe you have a dinosaur,

or a soft, snuggly monkey.

Or maybe you like to hug
a special pillow or a blanket.
Sometimes,
having a "bedtime buddy"
helps you feel safe
and ready to sleep.

We can snuggle up
with God's Word, too.
His Word will help us sleep.

The Bible says,*

"I can lie down

and go to sleep.

And I will wake up again

because the Lord protects me."

If you have a hard time

going to sleep,

remember this verse.

Learn it by heart.

Even when you are older,

God's Word can always be

your bedtime buddy!

*Psalm 3:5

A Verse to Learn

✪ I go to bed and sleep in peace.
Lord, only you keep me safe.
Psalm 4:8

A Story to Read

✪ "A Pillow and a Promise"
on page 50 of *The Young Reader's Bible,*
or
✪ Genesis 28:10-15

Something to Pray

✪ Ask God for help to learn his Word
so it will be your bedtime buddy.

Something to Do

✪ Copy Psalm 3:5 in a bright color. Keep it under
your pillow until you've learned it by heart.
✪ Find Psalm 121:3 in your Bible.

A Rainbow Around the Throne

To paint a rainbow,

you need lots of colors.

You need blue paint,

yellow, red, and green.

One color blends

into the next one.

The Bible tells us

that John saw a vision of heaven.

He saw a rainbow

around the throne of God.

It was the color of emeralds!

Angels were there, too,

singing praise to God and Jesus.

When we get to heaven,

we can look for the rainbow

and the angels

around God's throne.

But even better —

we will see Jesus!

With the angels,

we will sing praise to him.

We can join in singing,*

"Holy, holy, holy

is the Lord God All-Powerful.

He was, he is, and he is coming."

*Revelation 4:8

A Verse to Learn

☆ "Our Lord and God! You are worthy
to receive glory and honor and power."
Revelation 4:11

A Story to Read

☆ "Come Quickly, Lord Jesus!"
on page 430 of *The Young Reader's Bible,*
or
☆ Revelation 4:1-11

Something to Pray

☆ Tell Jesus how glad you will be to see him
face to face in heaven someday!

Something to Do

☆ Paint a picture of a rainbow.
☆ Paint a picture of what you think
heaven looks like.

Riding Free

When you first

begin to ride

a two-wheeled bike,

it is hard.

It is not easy.

It is work!

But once you learn to ride,

you can ride fast.

You can ride far.

You can ride much farther

than on your old tricycle.

You are free to ride

down the street

(with your parents' OK).

My Journal Pages

My Journal Pages

My Journal Pages

_____

_____

_____

_____

_____

_____

_____

_____

_____

_____

218

My Journal Pages

My Journal Pages

_____

_____

_____

_____

_____

_____

_____

_____

_____

_____

My Journal Pages

_____

_____

_____

_____

_____

_____

_____

_____

_____

_____

Devotions by Topic

To the Parent

    This book is designed to help your child develop a lifetime pattern of daily Bible reading and quiet time.

    There are devotions for Christmas, Easter, birthdays, school beginnings, and other holidays. Many of the devotions relate everyday experiences in a child's life to the Bible. In others, godly characteristics of Bible men and women provide positive role models. The accompanying lists on these two pages can help you meet your child's special needs.

    Each devotion can be completed over the course of one week. Read pages 4 and 5 with your child to help him see how to do the devotion in small sections. (If it's already bedtime and there's no time to try the "Something to Do" section, for example, plan to set aside time the next day.) Some children will be eager to have a devotions time all by themselves. Others will want a parent to participate.

    My prayer is that using this book will spark excitement in your child for reading the Bible and applying it daily to his or her life!

— Janet M. Bair

Standard Publishing offers other items for Young Readers, too!